T0146642

Young Children's Math and English Book with Illustrations.

Two Subjects in One Book for Students Both at Home and at School.

S. S. Fultang

authorHOUSE®

AuthorHouse™
1663 Liberty Drive
Bloomington, IN 47403
www.authorhouse.com
Phone: 1 (800) 839-8640

Published by AuthorHouse 09/01/2015

ISBN: 978-1-5049-4737-4 (sc)
ISBN: 978-1-5049-4738-1 (e)

Library of Congress Control Number: 2015914451

Print information available on the last page.

Contents

<u>Acknowledgement</u>

My family, my children Phile, Donald, Dad gave me a push to come forth with something as marvelous as this. Not forgetting my sisters Doris, - Gladys, Francis, Trina, Henry, George, Paulie & Doris edited the whole book.

I also give thanks to my parents, Mr. and Mrs Peter Fultang who educated me and supported me on this work. In all I am grateful for God for having gave me the ideas.

Chapter 1

Learn how to recognize numbers from 1 to 100.

1	2	3	4	5	6	7	8	9	10
11	12	13	14	15	16	17	18	19	20
21	22	23	24	25	26	27	28	29	30
31	32	33	34	35	36	37	38	39	40
41	42	43	44	45	46	47	48	49	50
51	52	53	54	55	56	57	58	59	60
61	62	63	64	65	66	67	68	69	70
71	72	73	74	75	76	77	78	79	80
81	82	83	84	85	86	87	88	89	90
91	92	93	94	95	96	97	98	99	100

Counting from 101 – 150

101	102	103	104	105	106
107	108	109	110	111	112
113	114	115	116	117	118
119	120	121	122	123	124
125	126	127	128	129	130
131	132	133	134	135	136
137	138	139	140	141	142
143	144	145	146	147	148
149	150				

<u>Complete the missing numbers</u>

1	2	3	4	_____
6	7	8	_____	10
11	12	13	_____	15
16	17	_____	19	20
_____	22	23	24	25
26	_____	28	29	_____
31	32	33	_____	35
36	37	38	39	_____

How many books are there?

1.   = _____

2.   = _____

3.   = _____

<u>Count and write the number of balls in each section.</u>

1. = _____

2. = _____

3. = _____

Count and write down the number of butterflies in each section

1.  =

2. =

3. =

Count the leaves on both sections and write the answer on the space

1.  =

2. =

3. =

4. =

Fill in the missing number

1   2   3   4   5   6   7   8   9   ____

11   12   ____   14   15   16   17   18   19   ____

21   22   23   24   25   ____   27   28   29   ____

31   32   33   ____   35   36   37   38   39   40

41   42   43   44   ____   46   47   48   49   ____

51   52   53   54   55   ____   57   58   59   ____

61   ____   63   64   65   66   ____   68   ____   ____

____   72   73   74   ____   76   77   78   79   80

Chapter 2

<   Stands for less than

>   Stands for greater than.

Examples

(a) 4 is less than 5
= 4 < 5

(b) 5 is greater than 3

= 5 > 3

Write > or <

a.   10   _____   5

b.   4   _____   8

c.   5   _____   2

d.   7   _____   10

e.   14   _____   13

f.   6   _____   5

g.   20   _____   10

h.   8   _____   7

i.   7   _____   5

j.   10   _____   9

k.   8   _____   15

l.   11   _____   12

Chapter 3

Numbers and their Spellings in words.

1 _____ one

2 _____ two

3 _____ three

4 _____ four

5 _____ five

6 _____ six

7 _____ seven

8 _____ eight

9 _____ nine

10 _____ ten

11 _____ eleven

12 _____ twelve

S. S. Fultang

Match these to their words

1	two
2	three
3	one
4	five
5	six
6	four
7	twelve
8	eight
9	seven
10	ten
11	eleven
12	nine

Chapter 4

Addition
Examples

Work these (sums) Problem

1. + =

2. + =

3. + =

4. $4 + 4 =$

5. $4 + 5 =$

6. $6 + 1 =$

7. $8 + 2 =$

8. $10 + 10 =$

Add these sums

a)   1 + 2 =

b)   3 + 1 =

c)   4 + 5 =

d)   5 + 4 =

e)   2 + 5 =

f)   5 + 2 =

g)   6 + 5 =

h)   1 + 6 =

i)   5 + 10 =

j)   9 + 9 =

k)   15 + 15 =

l)   19 + 19 =

Solve these sums

<u>Math</u>

1. $1 + 0 =$

2. $0 + 1 =$

3. $1 + 1 =$

4. $4 + 4 =$

5. $5 + 5 =$

6. $6 + 6 =$

7. $7 + 7 =$

8. $8 + 8 =$

9. $9 + 9 =$

10. $10 + 10 =$

11. $11 + 11 =$

Answers to choose from

Chapter 5

Tens and Units (T.U)

Examples - Place some numbers under the TU.

1.	10	=	T	U		
			1	0	& 1 Tenth - 1 Unit	

2.	12	=	T	U
			1	2

3.	92	=	T	U
			9	2

4.	24	=	T	U
			2	4

Addition of problems (sums) under T U

Examples

Add   10 + 11

a)   =   T   U
                 1   0
        +   1   1
        ─────────────────
                 2   1
        ─────────────────

                 T   U
                 1   0
        +   9
        ─────────────────
                 1   9
        ─────────────────

Add these sums

1.
```
      T   U
      2   5
  +   3   0
  _____
```

2.
```
      T   U
      4   0
  +   4   5
  _____
      8   5
```

3.
```
      T   U
      8   5
  +   1   0
  _____
```

4.
```
      T   U
      2   0
  +   1   0
  _____
```

Add these sums with carrying

<u>Examples:</u>

1.
```
    T  U
    8  5
+   1  9
-----------
1   0  4
-----------
```

2.
```
    T  U
    9  9
+      9
-----------
1   0
-----------
```

Work these sums

a)
```
    T  U
    2  9
+   2  9
-----------

-----------
```

b)
```
    T  U
    2  4
+   1  8
-----------

-----------
```

c)
```
    T  U
    5  8
+   1  4
-----------

-----------
```

d)
```
    T  U
    4  4
+   1  6
-----------

-----------
```

4)
```
    T  U
    3  5
+   9  5
-----------

-----------
```

5)
```
     T   U
         9
 +   2   3
 _____
```

6)
```
     T   U
     8   8
 +   2   5
 _____
```

7)
```
     T   U
     5   3
 +   4   8
 _____
```

8)
```
     T   U
     2   4
 +   1   9
 _____
```

Ex.1
```
     T   U
     1   5
 +   2   5
 _____
     4   0
```

Example 2

```
    ₁T   U
    ↓9  ↓8
 +       8
 _____
    10   6
```

Work out these

1)
```
     T   U
     8   2
 +   1   9
 _____
```

```
        T   U
        2   5
    +   6   9
    _____

        T   U
        5   8
    +   2   8
    _____
```

Ex.1
```
        T   U
        1   5
    +   2   5
    _____
        4   0
    _____
```

Example 2

```
       ₁T   U
        ↓9  ↓8
    +       8
    _____
       10   6
    _____
```

Work out these

1)
```
        T   U
        8   2
    +   1   9
    _____


        T   U
        2   5
    +   6   9
    _____


        T   U
        5   8
    +   2   8
    _____
```

Ex.1

T	U
1	5
+ 2	5
4	0

Example 2

	T	U
	₁	
	↓9	↓8
+		8
	10	6

Work out these

1)

T	U
8	2
+ 1	9

T	U
2	5
+ 6	9

T	U
5	8
+ 2	8

Work these subtraction sums under T.U

Example:

a)

T	U
↓2	↓8
- 1	5
1	3

23

1.
```
      T   U
      3   5
  -   1   1
  _____

  _____
```

2.
```
      T   U
      1   2
  -   1   1
  _____

  _____
```

3)
```
      T   U
      4   2
  -   2   1
  _____

  _____
```

4)
```
      T   U
      5   0
  -   1   0
  _____

  _____
```

5)
```
      T   U
      1   2
  -       2
  _____

  _____
```

Chapter 6

Arithmetic/Math

Additions with Carrying

Example: rough

            U   9 + 2 = 11

            T   4 + 5 + 1 = 10

            H   2 + 3 + 1 = 6

a)   H   T   U
            ↓2   ↓4   ↓9
       +   3   5   2
       _____
            6   0   1

Work these sums.

1.   H   T   U
            2   3   4
       +   4   9   2
       _____

2.   H   T   U
            8   2   9
       +   1   0   2
       _____

Addition with Carrying

Ex.1

	T	U
	1	5
+	2	5
	4	0

Chapter 6

Solving problems in words or worded problems

1. Carine has 10 bananas in one bowl and 5 bananas in another bowl. How many bananas are there?

2. I gave 2 cupcakes to my daughter and 4 to my son. How many did I give out?

3. In my school there are 10 girls in grade1 10 girls in grade 2. How many girls are in both classes?

Worded problems - Work them out,

1. In grade 5 the are 97 children, in grade 4, there are 25 children. How many children are there all together?

2. A trader puts 89 oranges in a big bag. The next day, he added 4 oranges to it. How many oranges are in there all together?

3. A piece of land has 35 trees planted. Then the farmer decides to plant 55 more trees. How many are the trees?

Addition

1. Add 259 bananas and 343 bananas. What is the answer?

2. I have 568 oranges. My Dad gave me 235 more oranges. How many oranges do I have now?

3. Our school library has 375 books. The school principal added 175 books. How many books are there together?

Ex.1

```
      T   U
      1   5
  +   2   5
  _____
      4   0
```

Example 2

```
     ₁T   U
     ↓9  ↓8
  +       8
  _____
     10   6
```

Work out these

1)
```
      T   U
      8   2
  +   1   9
  _____

```

```
      T   U
      2   5
  +   6   9
  _____

```

```
      T   U
      5   8
  +   2   8
  _____

```

Subtract these sums

1.   1 - 1 = 0

2.   2 - 1 =

3.   3 - 2 =

4.   6 - 3 =

5.   10 - 2 =

Subtraction

Complete these work.

1. 3 - 2 =

2. 4 - 3 =

3. 5 - 5 =

4. 6 - 1 =

5. 7 - 3 =

6. 8 - 3 =

7. 7 - 3 =

8. 8 - 3 =

9. 9 - 2 =

10. 6 - 5 =

11. 9 - 5 =

12. 8 - 7 =

13. 20 - 12 =

14. 10 - 10 =

15. 12 - 2 =

16. 12 - 10 =

Subtract these sums

1.
```
    T  U
    8  8
-   2  2
_____
```

2.
```
    T  U
    7  3
-   4  2
_____
```

3.
```
    T  U
    9  9
-   2  5
_____
```

4.
```
    T  U
    8  8
-   4  9
_____
```

5.
```
    T  U
    8  6
-   5  3
_____
```

6.
```
    T  U
    7  5
-   5  2
_____
```

Subtraction with borrowing

5 - 6
Borrow 1 from 7 and to the U. becomes 15 - 6 = 9, T becomes 6 - 1 = 5

```
      T   U
     ₆7  ¹5
  -   1   6
  _____
      5   9
```

1)
```
      T   U
      7   1
  -   2   6
  _____

```

2)
```
      T   U
      8   1
  -   2   5
  _____

```

3)
```
      T   U
      1   8
  -       9
  _____

```

4)
```
      T   U
      3   6
  -   2   3
  _____

```

Chapter 7

Multiplication tables

Learn to sing by heart!

<u>2 × tables</u>   How formed

2×1 = $\boxed{2}$ $= 2 + 0 = 2$

2×2 = $\boxed{4}$ $= 2 + 2 = 4$

2×3 = $\boxed{6}$ $= 2 + 2 + 2 = 6$

2×4 = $\boxed{8}$ $= 2 + 2 + 2 + 2 = 8$

2×5 = $\boxed{10}$ $= 2 + 2 + 2 + 2 + 2 = 10$

2×6 = $\boxed{12}$ $= 2 + 2 + 2 + 2 + 2 + 2 = 12$

2×7 = $\boxed{14}$ $= 2 + 2 + 2 + 2 + 2 + 2 + 2 = 14$

2×8 = $\boxed{16}$ $= 2 + 2 + 2 + 2 + 2 + 2 + 2 + 2 = 16$

2×9 = $\boxed{18}$

2×10 = $\boxed{20}$

2×11 = $\boxed{22}$

2×12 = $\boxed{24}$

3 times table

$3 \times 1 \quad = \quad \boxed{3}$

$3 \times 2 \quad = \quad \boxed{6}$

$3 \times 3 \quad = \quad \boxed{9}$

$3 \times 4 \quad = \quad \boxed{12}$

$3 \times 5 \quad = \quad \boxed{15}$

$3 \times 6 \quad = \quad \boxed{18}$

$3 \times 7 \quad = \quad \boxed{21}$

$3 \times 8 \quad = \quad \boxed{24}$

$3 \times 9 \quad = \quad \boxed{27}$

$3 \times 10 \quad = \quad \boxed{30}$

$3 \times 11 \quad = \quad \boxed{33}$

$3 \times 12 \quad = \quad \boxed{36}$

4 times table

4×1 = | 4 |

4×2 = | 8 |

4×3 = | 12 |

4×4 = | 16 |

4×5 = | 20 |

4×6 = | 24 |

4×7 = | 28 |

4×8 = | 32 |

4×9 = | 36 |

4×10 = | 40 |

4×11 = | 44 |

4×12 = | 48 |

5 times table

$5 \times 1 \quad = \quad \boxed{5}$

$5 \times 2 \quad = \quad \boxed{10}$

$5 \times 3 \quad = \quad \boxed{15}$

$5 \times 4 \quad = \quad \boxed{20}$

$5 \times 5 \quad = \quad \boxed{25}$

$5 \times 6 \quad = \quad \boxed{30}$

$5 \times 7 \quad = \quad \boxed{35}$

$5 \times 8 \quad = \quad \boxed{40}$

$5 \times 9 \quad = \quad \boxed{45}$

$5 \times 10 \quad = \quad \boxed{50}$

$5 \times 11 \quad = \quad \boxed{55}$

$5 \times 12 \quad = \quad \boxed{60}$

6 times table

$6 \times 1 \quad = \quad \boxed{6}$

$6 \times 2 \quad = \quad \boxed{12}$

$6 \times 3 \quad = \quad \boxed{18}$

$6 \times 4 \quad = \quad \boxed{24}$

$6 \times 5 \quad = \quad \boxed{30}$

$6 \times 6 \quad = \quad \boxed{36}$

$6 \times 7 \quad = \quad \boxed{42}$

$6 \times 8 \quad = \quad \boxed{48}$

$6 \times 9 \quad = \quad \boxed{54}$

$6 \times 10 \quad = \quad \boxed{60}$

$6 \times 11 \quad = \quad \boxed{66}$

$6 \times 12 \quad = \quad \boxed{72}$

<u>7 times table</u>

$7 \times 1 \quad = \quad \boxed{7}$

$7 \times 2 \quad = \quad \boxed{14}$

$7 \times 3 \quad = \quad \boxed{21}$

$7 \times 4 \quad = \quad \boxed{28}$

$7 \times 5 \quad = \quad \boxed{35}$

$7 \times 6 \quad = \quad \boxed{42}$

$7 \times 7 \quad = \quad \boxed{49}$

$7 \times 8 \quad = \quad \boxed{56}$

$7 \times 9 \quad = \quad \boxed{63}$

$7 \times 10 \quad = \quad \boxed{70}$

$7 \times 11 \quad = \quad \boxed{77}$

$7 \times 12 \quad = \quad \boxed{84}$

S. S. Fultang

8 times table

8 × 1 = 8

8 × 2 = 16

8 × 3 = 24

8 × 4 = 32

8 × 5 = 40

8 × 6 = 48

8 × 7 = 56

8 × 8 = 64

8 × 9 = 72

8 × 10 = 80

8 × 11 = 88

8 × 12 = 96

9 times table

$9 \times 1 \quad = \quad \boxed{9}$

$9 \times 2 \quad = \quad \boxed{18}$

$9 \times 3 \quad = \quad \boxed{27}$

$9 \times 4 \quad = \quad \boxed{36}$

$9 \times 5 \quad = \quad \boxed{45}$

$9 \times 6 \quad = \quad \boxed{54}$

$9 \times 7 \quad = \quad \boxed{63}$

$9 \times 8 \quad = \quad \boxed{72}$

$9 \times 9 \quad = \quad \boxed{81}$

$9 \times 10 \quad = \quad \boxed{90}$

$9 \times 11 \quad = \quad \boxed{99}$

$9 \times 12 \quad = \quad \boxed{108}$

10 times table

$10 \times 1 \quad = \quad \boxed{10}$

$10 \times 2 \quad = \quad \boxed{20}$

$10 \times 3 \quad = \quad \boxed{30}$

$10 \times 4 \quad = \quad \boxed{40}$

$10 \times 5 \quad = \quad \boxed{50}$

$10 \times 6 \quad = \quad \boxed{60}$

$10 \times 7 \quad = \quad \boxed{70}$

$10 \times 8 \quad = \quad \boxed{80}$

$10 \times 9 \quad = \quad \boxed{90}$

$10 \times 10 \quad = \quad \boxed{100}$

$10 \times 11 \quad = \quad \boxed{110}$

$10 \times 12 \quad = \quad \boxed{120}$

11 times table

$11 \times 1 \quad = \quad \boxed{11}$

$11 \times 2 \quad = \quad \boxed{22}$

$11 \times 3 \quad = \quad \boxed{33}$

$11 \times 4 \quad = \quad \boxed{44}$

$11 \times 5 \quad = \quad \boxed{55}$

$11 \times 6 \quad = \quad \boxed{66}$

$11 \times 7 \quad = \quad \boxed{77}$

$11 \times 8 \quad = \quad \boxed{88}$

$11 \times 9 \quad = \quad \boxed{99}$

$11 \times 10 \quad = \quad \boxed{110}$

$11 \times 11 \quad = \quad \boxed{121}$

$11 \times 12 \quad = \quad \boxed{132}$

12 times table

$12 \times 1 \quad = \quad \boxed{12}$

$12 \times 2 \quad = \quad \boxed{24}$

$12 \times 3 \quad = \quad \boxed{36}$

$12 \times 4 \quad = \quad \boxed{48}$

$12 \times 5 \quad = \quad \boxed{60}$

$12 \times 6 \quad = \quad \boxed{72}$

$12 \times 7 \quad = \quad \boxed{84}$

$12 \times 8 \quad = \quad \boxed{96}$

$12 \times 9 \quad = \quad \boxed{108}$

$12 \times 10 \quad = \quad \boxed{120}$

$12 \times 11 \quad = \quad \boxed{132}$

$12 \times 12 \quad = \quad \boxed{144}$

Chapter 8

Shapes

Square	Cube or Dice
Rectangle	
Triangle	Cylinder Prism
Circle	
Semi-circle	

Draw the following

a) Square

b) Rectangle

c) triangle

d) semi circle

Answer these questions

1. 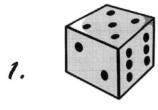 This is a _____

2.  This is a _____

3. This is a _____

S. S. Fultang

<u>Short multiplication with carrying</u>

ex.

```
   ₂T  U
   ᵦ2  ₐ5
 ×      5
 ─────────
   1  2  5
```

<u>Work out these</u>

1)
```
    T   U
    3   9
 ×      2
 ─────────
 
 ─────────
```

2)
```
    T   U
    2   6
 ×      2
 ─────────

 ─────────
```

3)
```
    T   U
    1   6
 ×      2
 ─────────

 ─────────
```

4)
```
    T   U
    1   8
 ×      2
 ─────────

 ─────────
```

5)
```
    T   U
    4   8
 ×      3
 ─────────

 ─────────
```

Work out this multiplication

1)
```
      T   U
      2   1
  ×       2
  _____

  _____
```

2)
```
      T   U
      2   2
  ×       2
  _____

  _____
```

3)
```
      T   U
      1   1
  ×       3
  _____

  _____
```

4)
```
      T   U
      1   1
  ×       4
  _____

  _____
```

5)
```
      T   U
      2   2
  ×       4
  _____

  _____
```

6)
```
      T   U
      3   3
  ×       2
  _____

  _____
```

Short multiplication with carrying

ex.

```
      ₂T   U
      ᵦ2  ₐ5
   ×       5
   ─────────
     1  2   5
```

Work out these

1)
```
      T   U
      3   9
   ×      2
   ────────
```

2)
```
      T   U
      2   6
   ×      2
   ────────
```

3)
```
      T   U
      1   6
   ×      2
   ────────
```

4)
```
      T   U
      1   8
   ×      2
   ────────
```

5)
```
      T   U
      4   8
   ×      3
   ────────
```

Short multiplication

1.

H	T	U
1	8	2
×		5
9	1	0

2.

H	T	U
1	1	2
×		4
4	4	8

Work these sums

1)

H	T	U
1	5	8
×		4

2)

H	T	U
8	1	1
×		2

S. S. Fultang

Addition under H.T.U

1.
H	T	U
↓2	↓2	↓5
+ 1	2	3
3	4	8

Work these sums

H	T	U
2	9	2
+ 2	6	1

H	T	U
4	9	8
+ 6	9	1

H	T	U
3	4	5
+ 2	4	2

Chapter 9

Long Multiplication

1)

```
      H   T   U
      1   9   2
  ×       1   2
 ─────────────────
  1   9   2   0
+     3   8   4
 ─────────────────
  2   3   1   4
```

2)

```
      H   T   U
      2   0   5
  ×       1   1
 ─────────────────
  2   0   5   0
+     2   0   5
 ─────────────────
  2   2   5   5
```

Solve these sums

1)

```
      H   T   U
      7   2   1
  ×       2   2
 ─────────────────

 ─────────────────
```

2)

```
      H   T   U
      1   8   5
  ×       3   5
 ─────────────────

 ─────────────────
```

Chapter 10

Division (sharing) ÷

1.) If 2 girls share 10 candies equally. What will each of them have?

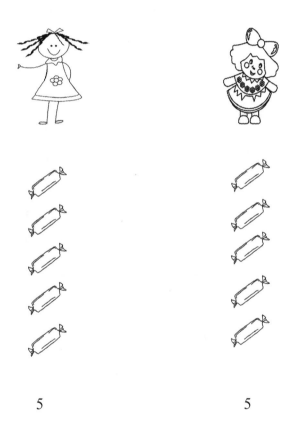

5   5

Division

Work these sums

1. $9 \div 4$ = [   ]

2. $7 \div 3$ = [   ]

3. $11 \div 2$ = [   ]

4. $8 \div 5$ = [   ]

5. $10 \div 7$ = [   ]

6. $11 \div 5$ = [   ]

7. $9 \div 2$ = [   ]

8. $5 \div 2$ = [   ]

9. $15 \div 4$ = [   ]

10. $20 \div 6$ = [   ]

11. $31 \div 5$ = [   ]

12. $25 \div 2$ = [   ]

Short Division

1.

   3 | 33

2.

   2 | 24

3.

   2 | 44

4.

   2 | 46

5.

   2 | 28

Short Division

Work these sums

1.

   2 $\overline{\smash{)}28}$ 3 $\overline{\smash{)}845}$

2.

   2 $\overline{\smash{)}45}$ 3 $\overline{\smash{)}941}$

3.

   3 $\overline{\smash{)}49}$ 3 $\overline{\smash{)}751}$

4.

   5 $\overline{\smash{)}75}$ 2 $\overline{\smash{)}85}$

5.

   3 $\overline{\smash{)}35}$ 9 $\overline{\smash{)}45}$

Long Division

Examples

1.

```
         44
     ┌─────
  2  │  88
     │  -8
     ├─────
     │  08
     │  08
     ├─────
     │  00
```

Ans = 44

2.

```
         31
     ┌─────
  3  │  93
     │  -3
     ├─────
     │  03
     │  03
     ├─────
     │  00
```

Ans = 31

Long Division - Solve these problems

1.

   3 | 22

2.

   5 | 35

3.

   3 | 66

4.

   5 | 25

5.

   2 | 24

Chapter 11

Work these sums here
in <u>Subtraction</u>

1)

H	T	U
↓2	↓8	↓9
- 1	2	5
1	6	4

1)

H	T	U
3	9	5
- 2	5	9

2)

H	T	U
8	9	0
- 2	5	0

3)

H	T	U
8	9	0
- 2	5	0

4)

H	T	U
8	8	7
- 7	9	9

Worded problems on subtraction.

1. If my mom gives me 150 dollars to bring bag 100 dollars to her. How much will you bring to her?

2. There were 500 oranges in a bag. If the trader sold 50. How much will be left?

3. I have 20 eggs and I gave 10 to my sister. How many are left with you?

Chapter 12

Calendar and date

AUGUST 2014						
Monday	Tuesday	Wednesday	Thursday	Friday	Saturday	Sunday
				1	2	3
4	5	6	7	8	9	10
11	12	13	14	15	16	17
18	19	20	21	22	23	24
25	26	27	28	29	30	31

Rhyme on days of the Month

30 days has September April June and November.
All the rest has 31 excepting February alone which
has but 28 and 29 days in a leap year.

Names of Months of the Year

	Months	Number of Days
1	January	_____ days
2	February	_____
3	March	_____
4	April	_____
5	May	_____
6	June	_____
7	July	_____
8	August	_____
9	September	_____
10	October	_____
11	November	_____
12	December	_____

Days of the weeks

1) Monday

2) Tuesday

3) Wednesday

4) Thursday

5) Friday

6) Saturday

7) Sunday

Calendar/date

1) 1) How many days are in 1 week?

2) 2) How many days are in 2 weeks?

3) 3) The first day of the week is called _____(Sunday, Monday).

4) 4) How many weeks in one month?

5) 5) How many days are in June?<u>Answer these questions</u>

1. 60 mins are equal _____ hour

2. How hours make one day. _____ hours

Chapter 13

Currency of the USA

Types or kinds of money in USA is made of

a) 100 dollars

b) 50 dollars

c) 20 dollars

e) 10 dollars

f) 5 dollars

g) quarter 25 cents

h) dime 10 cents

i) nickel 5 cents

j) penny 1 cent

<u>U.S. Currency</u>

Answer this questions

(1) How many cents (pennies) are in a nickel?

(2) How many cents are in a quarter?

(3) How many 1 dollars are in 5 dollars

(4) How many 50 dollars in 100 dollars?

(5) How many quarters make a dollar?

(6) If you add together 3 quarters. What will be the answer?

Chapter 14

<u>Fractions</u> - Introduction

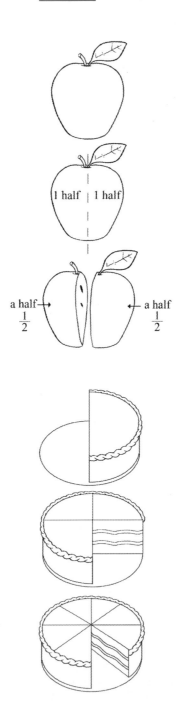

1 half 1 half

a half→
$\frac{1}{2}$

←a half
$\frac{1}{2}$

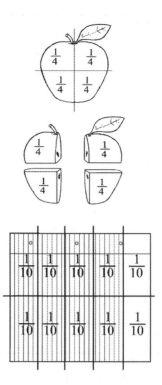

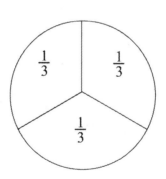

Draw a diagram to show

1.   ½

2.   1/5

3.   1/6

4.   2/5

Which is bigger ½ or 1/10?

$$\frac{1}{10} \quad \begin{array}{l} \text{- numerator} \\ \text{- denominator} \end{array}$$

Addition

1.
$$\frac{\frac{1}{2} \; + \; \frac{1}{2}}{\dfrac{1 \; + \; 1}{2}} \quad = 2/2 = 1$$

2. =
$$\frac{\frac{1}{2} \; + \; \frac{1}{2} \; + \; \frac{1}{2}}{\dfrac{1 \; + \; 1 \; + \; 1}{2}} \quad = \quad 3/2 = 1\,\frac{1}{2}$$

$$\frac{1+1+1}{2} = \frac{3}{2} = 1\tfrac{1}{2}$$

= 1 orange and half

Work out this fraction sums

1) $\frac{1}{2}$ + $\frac{1}{4}$ =

2) $\frac{1}{3}$ +   2/5   =

3)   1/5   +   4/8   =

4)   1/20   + $\frac{1}{4}$ =

Chapter 15

Telling/Reading the time

To  Past

- The time on this clock is 5 minutes past 12 noon.

- Clock hands

  ↗ Short hand reads the hours   ↗ Long hand read minutes past or to.

Read and write down the time on this clock

Chapter 16

Even Numbers/counting in 2's

2,	4,	6,	8,	10,	12,	14,	16,	18,	20
22,	24,	26,	28,	30,	32,	34,	36,	38,	40,
42,	44,	46,	48,	50,	52,	54,	56,	58,	60
-	-	-	-	-	-	-	-	-	-

to 100 and infinite

Counting Odd numbers are divided by 2 and with a remainder

1	3	5	7	9	11	13	15	17	19
21	23	25	27	29	-	-	-	-	-

and infinite - -

Contents

English

Letters of the alphabet

Small letters.

a   b   c   d   e   f   g   h   i   j   k

l   m   n   o   p   q   r   s   t   u   v

w   x   y   z

Capital letters of the alphabet

A   B   C   D   E   F   G   H   I   J   K

L   M   N   O   P   Q   R   S   T   U   V

W   X   Y   Z

Complete the capital and small letters

Aa   Bb   Cc   Dd   ☐   Ff   Gg

Hh   Ii   ☐   Kk   Ll   Mm   ☐

Oo   Pp   ☐   Rr   Ss   ☐   Uu

☐   Ww   Xx   Yy   ☐

Complete the missing letters of the alphabet

A__   Bb   C__   Dd   E__

__f   G__   H__   Ii   Jj

__k   Ll   M__   Nn   Oo

Pp   Qq   Uu   Vv   Ww

X__   Y__   Zz

S. S. Fultang

Match these letters to their small letters

Capital	Small letters
A	b
B	a
C	d
D	c
E	f
F	e
G	h
H	g
I	j
J	i
K	l
L	k
M	m

Chapter 2

Some words that begin with the same letter of the alphabet

f

a ------------ animal

b ------------ banana

c ------------ cat

d ------------ dog

e ------------ elephant

f ------------ fish

k   -   kite ——————   **g** ------------- **girl**

                          h ------------- **hat**

                          i ------------- **igloo**

                          j ------------- **jacket**

                          k ------------- **kite**

u   -   umbrella ——————   **l** ------------- **leg**

                          m ------------- **milk**

                          n ------------- **nine**

                          o ------------- **orange**

                          p ------------- **pig**

z   -   zip —————— q ------------ **queen**

r ------------ **run**

s ------------ **sun**

t ------------ **tree**

u ------------ **umbrella**

v ------------ **violin**

w ------------ **wings**

x ------------ **xylophone**

y ------------ **yarn**

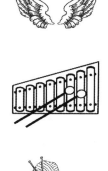

z ------------ **zipper**

Match the letters to the objects that begin with that letter.

Chapter 3

road

table

flowers

bed

house

igloo

zipper

pen

ball

nine

tree

girl

kite

leg

Study the picture and word

Learn to spell the word.

man

woman

boy

girl

Mom is cooking

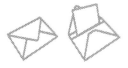

Airplane

Envelope

Young Children's Math and English Book with Illustrations.

Complete these spellings   **Choose the right letter to complete**

1.   fis___   l

2.   h___t   h

3.  ba___l   a

4.  ca___d   g

5.   pi___   o

6.   pe___   r

7.   bo___k   t

8.   ki___e   n

Underline the correct word.

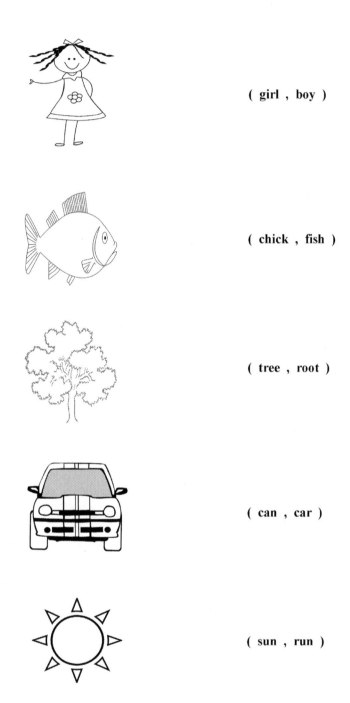

(girl , boy)

(chick , fish)

(tree , root)

(can , car)

(sun , run)

Chapter 4

Verbs is an action word in a sentence. Draw the action.

<u>Some verbs</u>

1. | play

2. | stand

3. | kneel

4. | eat

5. | sit

6. | run

7. | go

8. | come

9. | look

10. | open

B.   <u>To have</u>

I	have
You	have
She/he	has
We	have
They	have

C.   <u>To go</u>

I	go
You	go
She/he	goes
We	go
They	go

(Samples) Everyday speech verbs conjugates

A)   <u>To be</u>

I	am
You	are
She/he	is
We	are
You	are
They	are

(Samples) Everyday speech verbs conjugates

Complete by underlining the best answers.

1. I (<u>has, have</u>) a big toy car.

2. She (has, have), a green book in her hand.

3. They all (has, have) bags.

4. I (go, goes) to school in a school bus.

5. She (goes, go) to visit her parents every week-end.

6. We (are, am) all tall.

7. I (am, have) a cute girl.

Tenses

No.	Present continuous tense	Present tense	Past tense	Future tense	Past perfect tense
	Now	Everyday	Yesterday	Tomorrow	Last time
1.	I am eating	I eat	I ate	I shall eat	I had eaten
2.	I am running	I run	I ran	I shall run	I had run
3.	I am sitting	I sit	I sat	I shall sit	I had walk
4.	I am walking	I walk	I walked	I shall walk	I had walked
5.	I am writing	I write	I wrote	I shall write	I had written
6.	I am going	I go	I went	I shall go	I had gone
7.	I am talking	I talk	I talked	I shall talk	I had talked
8.	I am taking	I take	I took	I shall take	I had taken
9.	I am coming	I come	I came	I shall come	I had come
10.	I am crying	I cry	I cried	I shall cry	I had cried
11.	I am buying	I buy	I bought	I shall buy	I had bought

Fill in the spaces with the right answers.

1.) I [_____] my bag to school, yesterday.

2.) Whenever I am [_____] I drink water. (tired, tire)

3.) That man who [_____] to our house this morning was my father's friend.

4.) I [_____] to school every day (walk, sit).

5.) My mum [_____] at the post office (work, walk).

6.) I [____] here (is, am, there)

7.) My Dad is a (man, girl)

8.) He takes a good

Chapter 5

He is climbing a _____. (tree, three)

He is reading a book, (on, a) _____ table

They are _____ to school. (school, going)

The girl is sleeping on the _____.

Complete these sentence with the right spellings

1. This is a .   fi___h

2. John is .   run___ing

3. The is under the table.   ba___l

4. This is a .   ca___dy

5. My mom goes to on Sunday to pray.   ch___rch

6. is sweet.   ban___ana.

7. It is outside.   ra___ning

8. This is a pair of .   sh___es.

Choose the right letter to complete the spellings

Words	Letters
1) Ma__	o
2) b__y	n
3) girl__	i
4) wo__an	a
5) Th__s	s
6) D__d	m
7) M__m	o

Chapter 6

picture

shirt

bottle

ruler

Young Children's Math and English Book with Illustrations.

<u>Test</u>

Complete these questions

1. This is a _____.

2. This is a _____.

3. This is a _____.

4. This is a _____.

5. This is a _____.

6. This is a _____.

7. This is a _____.

8. This is a _____.

John is going to school.

My dad is reading a newspaper.

The ball is round.

Chapter 7

<u>Learn to spell these words.</u>

1. it

2. is

3. on

4. in

5. of

6. an

7. or

8. to

9. he

10. am

11. we

12. go

13. by

14. she

Complete by choosing the right word

1. _____ is a mango. (on, or, it)

2. This _____ a big pear (it, on, is)

3. My bag is _____ the table (it, up, on)

4. My friend is _____ (by, of, in) the house.

5. The bird is sitting the tree (it, to, on) the tree.

6. _____ orange is sweater than a plum, (he, am, an)

7. A half _____ the banana is bad (is, he, of)

8. Please give me a pen _____ a pencil the write with

9. I go _____ school everyday.

10. _____ is a boy. (she, he, I)

Complete by choosing the right word

Chapter 8

Words & Plurals

Words   Plurals

one pen   two pens

one book   two books

one apple   two apples

one boy   two boys

Write down the plurals of these words by simply adding an (s) to the singulars

Singulars	Plurals
1. pencil	pencil<u>s</u>
2. boy	boy<u>s</u>
3. girl	girl<u>s</u>
4. car	car<u>s</u>
5. tree	tree<u>s</u>
6. picture	picture_
7. bed	bed_
8. cat	cat_
9. book	book_
10. cap	cap_
11. shoe	shoe_
12. bag	bag_
13. comb	comb
14. phone	phone

Write plurals of these words (add s).

1. fan — ☐

2. shirt — ☐

3. spoon — ☐

4. fork — ☐

5. house — ☐

6. plate — ☐

7. bowl — ☐

8. ball — ☐

9. backpack — backpacks

10. television — televisions

11. chair — ch--

12. trouser — ☐

13. door — ☐

Plurals that end with $\boxed{y}$ just replace the $\boxed{y}$ with a $\boxed{ies}$

Words (Singular)	Plurals
1. Lorry	Lorr $\boxed{ies}$
2. worry	worr $\boxed{ies}$
3. baby	
4. lady	
5. family	
6. fly	
7. fry	
8. lady	

Plurals of words that end in ch/sh just add es at the end of the word.

Words	Plurals
1. church	
2. brush	
3. bench	
4. couch	
5. bush	
6. match	
7. watch	
8. coach	
9. branch	
10. calabash	
11. torch	

More irregular plurals

Words	Plurals
1. man	
2. woman	
3. tooth	
4. child	
5. person	
6. fish	
7. louse	

Words whose spellings end w/ <u>o</u>, the plural becomes es, you just add $\boxed{es}$

Words	Plurals
1. mango	
2. tomato	
3. echo	

S. S. Fultang

Plurals that do not end with an (s). There are called irregular plural

Words or nouns that end, in f, you just take out f, and replace with ves.

Words	Plurals that end in f
1. wife	wives
2. knife	knives
3. calf	calves
4. loaf	

Chapter 9

<u>Underline the right answer</u>

I wash my hands before and after _____. (eating , sitting)

They _____ (are, am) watchign TV.

I brush _____ (for , my) teeth everyday.

I am _____. (running , standing)

I am _____. (running , standing)

I am _____. (sitting , climbing)

I am _____. (sitting , climbing)

Irregular verbs and past tense

Verbs (words)		Past tense
1	cry	
2	write	
3	go	
4	come	
5	run	
6	sit	
7	read	
8	see	
9	buy	
10	teach	
11	steal	
12.	have	

Underline the right plurals that completes the sentences.

1. My mom uses many (tomatoes, toes) to cook.

2. (Children, Child) go to school to learn to read, write, and speak good English.

3. Some child care schools have many (baby, babies).

4. One of my (teeth, tooth) is hurting.

5. Some children put on (watches, watch) to school.

6. Everybody in my house uses a tooth (brush, brushes).

7. When I went out to shop at Walnut I found some (knives, knife).

8. This (plate, plates) is dirty.

9. In my city the tallest (church, churches) building is painted in blue and white.

10. My friends are mostly (girls, girl).

11. (Boys, Boy) like to wear caps.

12. My (backpack, backpacks) is full of books.

13. I can see two cows and their (calf, calves).

14. Most men get married to one (wife, wives)

15. I wash my (hand, hands) before eating.

Chapter 10

Antonyms opposites of words

	Words	Opposite
1	wet	dry
2	cold	hot
3	bad	good
4	rich	poor
5	kind	cruel
6	agree	oppose
7	come	go
8	heavy	light
9	oppose	support
10	clean	dirty
11	happy	sad
12	soft	hard
13	easy	difficult
14	rough	smooth
15	long	short
16	same	different

Write the opposites of these words

Words		Antonyms/opposites
1	dirty	_____
2	smooth	_____
3	sad	_____
4	hard	_____
5	difficult	_____
6	go	_____
7	dry	_____
8	hot	_____
9	cruel	_____
10	light	_____
11	dark	_____
12	oppose	_____
13	bad	_____

Chapter 11

Irregular verbs and past tenses

Verbs (words)	Past tenses
go	went
come	came
see	saw
run	ran
stand	stood
sit	sat
buy	bought
teach	taught
take	took
steal	stole
lie	lied
ride	rode
have	had
be	was
write	wrote
pay	paid
cry	cried

Chapter 12

Parts of the body

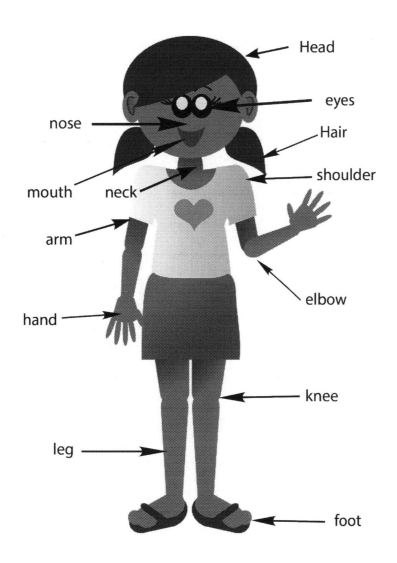

nose

mouth   neck

arm

hand

Head

eyes

Hair

shoulder

elbow

knee

leg

foot

The five senses are

1. eye _____   sight

2. ear _____   hearing

3. tongue _____   taste

4. touch _____   feeling

5. nose _____   smell

Colors

Draw a rainbow

1. Red

2. Blue

3. White

4. Black

5. Green

6. Yellow

7. Orange

8. Pink

9. Purple

10. Brown

Story - <u>The Cat and the Rat</u>

Once upon a time there were two friends, a cat and a rat. They loved themselves in such a way that they did everything together. The cat's friends became the rat's friends. They all lived like a big family.

One day their friends decided to have a party in an island. As they organized their party, they decided to invite their original friends. Therefore, both the cat and the rat were invited to this party. Even though they did everything together the cat discussed with the rat about the invitation.

"Hello, Rat, I have been invited to this party by the king of the forest. What do you think about it? Are you going to that party?"

"The Rat answered, I was invited for the same party. I was going to ask you to come with me to that party."

The cat answered, "Yes let's all go to the party. We have problem," he said while shaking his whiskers. "We both do not know how to swim". How shall we do? For a while he thought there was no way for them to go to this party, the rat thought for himself.

Suddenly he brightened up; I know how we can go to the party. We can go by boat. The cat didn't know how or where to get a boat. Then the Rat said, "we can fix our own boat."

The cat replied, "How shall we do that? You are not a carpenter and either am I. See tell me who can help us fix a boat on time for us to cross the river." The Rat said we can fix our boat by carving out a boat from a yam and other materials. The cat collected some sticks alongside some nails but no hammer. There was no way they could fix for themselves a boat. The rat suggested that they should take the yam and carve a hole within it using the sticks. The cat accepted and they put to work all the ideas. After some hours or hard labor they produced a boat. All what was left for them was to clean up themselves and get to the party. So the cat went to clean up himself while the rat too also did cleaned up.

The rat returned before the cat, then decided to taste some of the left over dirt. The dirt tasted so good in such a way that it was tempting just looking at the boat.

They both left for the party. At the party they were both having so much fun and the cat forgot that they had to take care of the boat. At the end of the party the cat went to get the boat but couldn't find it. Then he looked high and near for the Rat and he could not find him.

Up till today whenever the cat sees the rat he always goes after him. They became enemies rather than of friends.

Questions from the story

1. Who were friends?

2. Who invited them for a party?

3. What did they make a boat out of?

4. Where was the party?

5. Is the Cat and the Rat friends?

Preface

I decided to do this work on Fundamental Maths & English for the Junior grades because it is a foundation for their future program in Maths, and English. It is at this stage that if children are not well molded in Maths & English they will go astray and will dread Maths & English. If God does not lay the foundation of the house the laborers labored in vain.

Let us not skip over this.

Printed in the United States
By Bookmasters